W9-BNU-669

The Learning Resource Center

Hurlbutt Elementary School

DATE DUE

NOV 1			
JA 21 '03			
JE 18 '03			
MR 11 '03			
OC 22 '03			
OC 23 '03			
OC 1 04			

Demco

Animals with Jobs

Animal Actors

Judith Janda Presnall

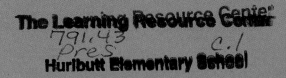

The Learning Resource Center

791.43
Pres

c.1

Hurlbutt Elementary School

KidHaven Press

KidHaven Press, an imprint of Gale Group, Inc.
10911 Technology Place, San Diego, CA 92127

For my family: Lance, Kaye, and Kory

Library of Congress Cataloging-in-Publication Data
Presnall, Judith Janda.
    Animal actors / by Judith Janda Presnall.
      p. cm. — (Animals with jobs)
    Includes bibliographical references.
    Summary: Discusses the use of animals in films and television, their training and care both on and off the set, and the American Humane Association's monitoring of their treatment.
    ISBN 0-7377-0934-0 (hardback : alk. paper)
    1. Animals in motion pictures. 2. Animals on television. [1. Animals in motion pictures. 2. Animals on television. 3. Working animals. 4. Animals—Training. 5. Animals—Treatment. 6. American Humane Association.] I. Title. II. Series.
    PN1995.9.A5 P74 2002
    791.43'662—dc21
    2001002181

Acknowledgments
The author wishes to thank the following people for reviewing her manuscript and for their helpful suggestions: Karen Rosa, American Humane Association, communications manager, Film & TV Unit, Sherman Oaks, California; Bob Dunn, owner of Bob Dunn's Animal Services, Sylmar, California.

Copyright © 2002 by KidHaven Press, an imprint of Gale Group, Inc.
10911 Technology Place, San Diego, CA 92127

No part of this book may be reproduced or used in any form or by any other means, electrical, mechanical, or otherwise, including, but not limited to, photocopying, recording, or any information storage and retrieval system, without prior written permission from the publisher.

Printed in the U.S.A.

Contents

Chapter One

Animal Actors: Present and Past

Animals are more popular in film and television today than ever before. For over one hundred years, a wide variety of critters have fascinated, terrified, and amused audiences in movies, on television, and on the stage. Animals can, and do, become big stars. Today's animal actors include a whale, dogs, and even small insects.

A Whale of a Story

The orca whale Keiko, who was made famous in the movies *Free Willy* and *Free Willy 2*, is probably the biggest animal actor, weighing in at about 7,720 pounds. The orca was captured and sold to two marine parks, the second one in Mexico City, where he was trained to respond to hand and arm gestures.

The goal was to **rehabilitate** Keiko so he could be healthy, learn to catch fish, and eventually be returned to the North Atlantic waters in Iceland where he was born. At the time of this writing, Keiko has been in Iceland since 1998 and has completed many exercises for his release and independence. Researchers have taught Keiko many tasks that orcas do for survival, such as learning to **gorge** and feast on fish, having encounters with other orcas (in hopes he will be accepted into a pod of whales), and deep diving.

A Mutt Superstar

Benji—a mixture of cocker spaniel, schnauzer, and poodle whose real name was Higgins—was rescued by trainer Frank Inn from a Burbank, California, animal

Researchers teach Keiko the skills necessary to survive in the ocean.

shelter. Inn taught Higgins one trick each week for thirty-nine weeks. The dog was steadily employed for eight years in a weekly television series. Higgins was known for his facial expressions that conveyed happiness, sadness, and even anger. At the age of thirteen (almost one hundred in human years), Higgins was chosen to be in the movie *Benji*.

Higgins sired many litters, creating several "mini" versions of himself. Benji II, Higgins's daughter, has appeared in several movies and television specials.

Air Bud

Another dog that audiences enjoyed was Buddy, a golden retriever who played basketball in a Disney movie entitled *Air Bud*. Complete with custom-made basketball shoes on his feet (for traction) and a team shirt, Buddy ended up sinking the winning free throws in the movie's finale.

Past Actors

In the 1950s horses were popular costars in Western movies and television shows. Each cowboy had his own special horse, and the horse was just as much of a star as the human. Roy Rogers had Trigger, Gene Autry had Champion, and the Lone Ranger had Silver. Combined, all three horses costarred in over 150 films and over 400 television episodes.

Two dogs, Rin Tin Tin and Lassie, paved the way for today's dogs to star in movies. Rin Tin Tin I, a German shepherd, made twenty-two movies. Later movies

Trigger the horse costarred in film and television episodes with Roy Rogers in the 1950s.

starred Rin Tin Tin II and III. The dynasty continued with Rin Tin Tin IV, and Rinty Jr. starring in the *Adventures of Rin Tin Tin* television series, which ran from 1954 to 1959.

Lassie was another dog that won audiences' hearts. The famous collie made seven movies. Although portrayed as a female, Lassie was actually a male named Pal. All of the collies that played Lassie were males because males are larger and have fuller coats. Lassie's son first appeared in six movies and then began starring in the TV series *Lassie*, which lasted nineteen years, ending in 1973. By the end of the series, five **generations** of Pal's family had portrayed Lassie.

The reason that the animals could continue in those roles for so long is because they handed their stardom down from generation to generation.

Rin Tin Tin, pictured above, and Lassie paved the road for dog movie stars.

Animal actors, like Lassie from the New Lassie TV series, receive special treatment on the job.

First-Class Treatment for Small Domestic Animals

Domestic animals are those that are tame and can live in a family home, such as dogs, cats, and birds. These animal actors often receive special treatment when they travel for their jobs. For example, normally airlines allow only guide dogs in the cabin of an airplane without being in a carrier. However, some airlines make exceptions for superstar canines.

Lassie traveled first class on airlines (a $2,400 ticket compared to $100 in the cargo compartment) and drank only bottled water. Lassie from the *New Lassie* syndicated television series flies under his own name, earns frequent-flier miles, and usually pays only half-fare since he's under twelve. Besides choice food during the day, Lassie also prefers to start the morning with a glazed doughnut.

Not all airlines will fly animals in a first-class seat. Once a Canadian airline forced an animal handler to rent out the entire first-class section in order to get his dog on board.

Animal actors also stay in ritzy hotels, have favorite rawhide bones, and eat specially prepared foods. Vans with side awnings, luxurious trailers, heated and cooled buildings, and sometimes a plot of land for exercise are all comforts provided for animal actors.

Salaries for Animal Actors in 2001

Animal actors get paid well, too. A grizzly bear is usually paid between $2,500 and $4,000 for a day's work. Other daily salaries include $500 for a **venomous** snake and $200 for a king snake. When he is not making a movie, Benji earns $10,000 for a personal appearance.

Sometimes the pay scale depends on the age of the animal. For example, a six-year-old chimpanzee earns $800 a day. However, because an adult chimpanzee is stronger, more difficult to handle, and requires a more experienced trainer, it will earn $1,200 a day. Some agencies take no less than $400 per day for any type of animal, even if it is a mouse. The fee covers insurance, traveling, and handling costs.

Adult chimpanzee actors, because they are strong and hard to handle, earn $1,200 a day.

Animals in Movies Affect Sales

Some animal actors motivate moviegoers to make unplanned purchases. After the *101 Dalmatians* and *102 Dalmatians* movies, sales of Dalmatian pups increased dramatically. Other items were boosted by the movie, such as Dalmatian-spotted clothing, stuffed toy dogs, and jewelry. In addition, fast-food restaurants add movie-related toys to their children's meal boxes to promote movies and to increase the restaurant's sales.

Chapter Two

Training Animal Actors

Whether in movies, television series, or commercials, almost every animal has been trained. Any well-trained animal can be a good actor. Good acting comes from steady **repetition** and hard work. Animal actors must learn to perform in strange locations, in front of many people, and under hot camera lights. A skilled trainer helps animal actors overcome these difficulties.

Trainers Make Animal Actors Stars

Just owning an extraordinary animal does not make the animal an actor. It is the trainer who makes the animal a star. The trainer recognizes an animal's talents, then works to develop them. Trainer Karl Lewis Miller says:

> There's no difference between a common house pet and an animal superstar except the trainers. . . . It's having an animal in the right place at the right time with the person who has the experience and the expertise to teach an animal to do it. An animal is as good or as bad as his trainer. Sure, there is something

Animal actors learn their trade from trainers.

special about the animal, but only because it's brought out by the person teaching him.[1]

Affection Training

These days most animal trainers use a gentle method of training called "affection training." This method uses love, patience, understanding, and respect.

Ralph Helfer started affection training when he founded Africa USA near Los Angeles, California, in the 1970s. Africa USA at one time housed fifteen hundred wild animals and retained a crew of keepers and trainers. Helfer supplied animal performers for over five thousand movies and television programs. Rather than use the old method of "fear" training, Helfer employed affection training.

Helfer gives this example:

> To really understand a bear, you have to "be" like a bear. Swimming with him, brushing his back,

Trainers rely on love, patience, understanding, and respect in teaching animals to act.

wrestling with him, sharing honey and watermelon with him, napping together under a tree. . . . Respect must be earned. When the animal has experienced your love, your patience, and your willingness to be understanding, you will have earned that animal's respect.[2]

Daily Training

Dogs are easiest to train because they have a strong desire to please. Training bears, horses, or pigs is more difficult because, unlike dogs, they do not want to please humans. A relationship with these animals is more difficult and takes longer.

Training an animal, whether for a difficult or simple task, requires consistency and time. For instance, when teaching a new trick to a dog, a trainer typically works with the dog five or ten minutes a day, *every* day, on that trick.

Jumping Through a Window

Trainers teach each individual movement of a stunt or trick separately. A scene that may only appear on the screen for thirty seconds may take an animal several days or even a year to learn.

Big Red, an Irish setter, had to learn several tricks for a Disney movie. One was to jump through a glass window. To meet this goal, trainer Bill Koehler followed several steps. First, he had the glass removed from the window and a ramp installed from the floor to the **sill.** Koehler placed Big Red on a "stay" command inside the house and crawled through the window while Big Red watched. When Koehler called, Big Red bounded through enthusiastically.

At the next training level, the crew hung a clear **vinyl** sheet over the window opening. Big Red first went through the opening slowly as he felt the vinyl brush his back. Finding that the vinyl gave way to his

Difficult moves require extra training.

forward movement, Big Red practiced lunging up the ramp and butting the vinyl aside to go through.

Next, the crew removed the ramp. As Big Red rehearsed leaping through the window, Koehler gave him a "down" and "on your side" command. Later the crew replaced the vinyl with a solid pane of breakaway glass— a safe, noncutting material. Koehler told Big Red to stay, then walked around and showed his face through the window so Big Red would focus on him. When filming began, Koehler walked out of camera range and called Big Red. The crew heard digging nails on the floor, silence while Big Red was airborne, and then "glass" spraying in all directions. Big Red obeyed the "down" command and crumpled to the floor on his side unharmed, successfully completing the stunt, which he had mastered in just two days, with only one camera take.

Working with Wild Animals

Dogs such as Big Red are easier to teach than wild animals. Behavior instruction for wild or **exotic animals** must start when they are babies or they cannot be trained. The trainer must first tame the animal. Then the trainer can coach it to be wild, but on command only.

The biggest danger in working with large wild animals such as lions, elephants, bears, and chimpanzees is that they sometimes do not behave. Even when the animal is trained, it can still turn on its trainer or a human actor.

Wild animals are first tamed and then taught how to act as they would in nature.

Grizzly Bears

Bears are considered among the most dangerous animals to train. They are eight times as strong as humans and have nasty tempers. Animal counselor Jean-Philippe Varin says, "It's easier to train a fish than to know what goes on in a bear's head."[3]

Trainer Doug Seus owns the Wasatch Wildlife Animal Training Center in Heber City, Utah, where he raised and trained Bart, an Alaskan Kodiak grizzly, from the age of five weeks. The cub weighed just five pounds when Seus took over his care. He played with Bart from the moment the bear woke up in the morning until he fell asleep at night.

The huge grizzly grew to be nine and a half feet tall and weighed fifteen hundred pounds. When Bart worked on *The Bear* film, his daily diet included five cans of British Columbia salmon, five pounds of apples and carrots, three loaves of bread, ten cans of berries, and six chickens; he also drank two quarts of milk and a cooler full of iced tea and Diet Coke.

The Bear

Before filming *The Bear,* the director listed behaviors that Bart had to learn, such as crawling on his belly, limping, and swiping live fish out of water. Seus's biggest challenge, however, was to teach Bart to accept his cub costar Douce. Bart had to be trained to be gentle to the cub.

To train Bart for this part, Seus sprinkled a stuffed teddy bear with Douce's urine and taught Bart to lift it gently, then hug and kiss it. After Bart was comfortable

Trainer Doug Seus gets a kiss from Bart the bear.

with the toy, Seus introduced Bart to Douce. This training took one year. During the six-month shoot, Bart and Douce performed on the set only three hours at a time, before becoming tired and cranky.

In his acting career, Bart appeared in fifteen feature films, eight TV productions, and sixteen documentaries. Since Bart's death at the age of twenty-three on May 10, 2000, two new cubs—Little Bart and Honey Bump at Wasatch Wildlife—are being trained to replace him.

Insect Stars

Not all animal actors are large furry animals. There is also a need for tiny bugs. Of course, insects and reptiles

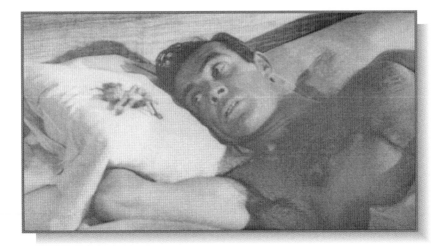

A tarantula appears in a James Bond movie.

cannot be trained like dogs or bears, but they still must follow the action called for in a script. Professional entomologists, people who study insects, sometimes are "bug wranglers," or trainers, on the side.

Bug wranglers supply insects for films—mostly horror and adventure movies—such as *Creepshow* and *Indiana Jones and the Temple of Doom. Indiana Jones*, for example, used 50,000 crickets, 12 long-horned beetles, 10 centipedes, and 5,000 cockroaches—supplied at a cost of $5,000.

Bug wranglers get the insects to do what the script requires by having the set built to accommodate the natural tendencies of the insects. For instance, if an insect likes to move toward light, lights are placed where the insects are supposed to go. Or the insect may be lured toward a food source. And as with all animal actors, many methods are used to protect them from harm.

Chapter Three

Animals on the Job

Animal actors often have to travel great distances for a film. Such was the case for *Sheena, Queen of the Jungle.* Hubert Wells, owner and head trainer of Animal Actors of Hollywood, flew two planeloads of animals to Africa. This strange cargo included an elephant, a rhino, four lions, three leopards, and four chimpanzees. As one animal trainer puts it, "You cannot just walk into the jungle and expect lions and leopards to turn up on the set to **audition.**"[4]

Movies may take a year to film. Nine months of that time is spent training the animal for its role before three months of actual filming.

How Animals Get Jobs

Many animal actor agencies supply studios with exotic as well as domestic animals. Most of the agencies are located in New York or California since filming is most common in or near these areas. Agencies also perform other services including training, scheduling jobs, and assigning personnel to accompany the animals to their jobs.

Several agencies, such as Bob Dunn's Animal Services in Sylmar, California, have a **compound** where most of their animal actors live. Dunn has obtained additional animals from breeders and other trainers

Hubert Wells's Animal Actors of Hollywood supplies studios with exotic animals.

Actor Clint Eastwood relaxes with his orangutan costar, "Clyde," while filming Any Which Way You Can.

worldwide. The agency can acquire any animal desired from butterflies to reptiles to apes or anything in between. Dunn has supplied orangutans and capuchin monkeys for both *Flintstones* movies; a chimpanzee for *Buddy*; skunks, rats, and chimpanzees for *Dr. Dolittle*; and a rhesus macaque monkey for *George of the Jungle*.

American Humane Association
Animal actors are protected by the American Humane Association (AHA), which is the official watchdog of

the film industry. They have set guidelines, which insure that animals are **humanely** treated and protected against injury, neglect, and abuse during filming. Those guidelines, along with today's creative technology, promise animal actors a safe working environment. Movie producers are obligated to notify AHA in advance if animals will be used in a production.

A Typical Day

A typical film shooting day, especially outdoors, starts at about five or six in the morning and ends when the sun disappears. The behind-the-scenes crew, as well as human actors and animal actors, must be ready to start at daybreak.

Preparation is more difficult for the animals. Before they even approach the set, they must be put "in the mood" by working with the trainer for about an hour. Then they must go to makeup. Humans concern themselves mostly with facial makeup. But animals must be made up all over. Their appearance must fit the action of the scene.

Makeup for Pigs

Even pigs must be made up. Every morning during the filming of both *Babe* and *Babe: Pig in the City*, the makeup crew washed the six working piglets, dyed their eyelashes black, and glued their distinctive cluster toupees in place. About eight hundred live critters performed in each *Babe* movie. Because pigs grow rapidly, one hundred white Yorkshire piglets—all females—played Babe.

One hundred white Yorkshire piglets played the star in the movie Babe.

For ten weeks, a team of seventeen handlers played with, bottle-fed, and trained a set of six piglets. Babe's head trainer, Joanne Kostiuk, named them. Each group of piglets' names began with the same letter of the alphabet. The first piglets, named Allie, Aggie, Annie, Abby, Angie, and Amy, were four weeks old when they started. Every batch of Babes could work for only three weeks before they grew too big for the part. In each group, the piglet with the most appealing personality played Babe. The remaining five piglets were stand-ins and stunt pigs. Before the movie ended, Kostiuk had worked her way to Quincy, Quigley, Queenie, Quattro, Qualley, and Quizzie.

Special Techniques

Some stunts seem dangerous to the viewer, but in actuality they are not. Scenes that appear dangerous but are actually created in safe, controlled environments are called "**simulated**," or pretend, scenes. Simulated action

Most movie stunts look dangerous but are carefully planned.

An animatronic iguana moves and looks like a live animal.

includes everything from techniques of film editing to realistic props to computer-generated images.

Filmmakers use a variety of clever tricks to protect the animal actors. One good example of a movie that applies multiple methods is *Dr. Dolittle.* Along with the large variety of live animal actors that appear in this comedy, the movie also uses special effects, such as animatronics, blue screen, split screen, and computerized digital technology.

In animatronics, a specially constructed stuffed animal that moves and appears alive replaces the live animal. This matching **animated** animal appears in scenes that would be too dangerous for the real animal. For example, in *Dr. Dolittle,* Rodney the pet guinea pig, Lucky the dog, as well as the rat, the owl, the tiger, and the pigeons, all had animatronic doubles. Many of the animals also had multiple live doubles, allowing them to rotate and rest often.

Special Screens

Filmmakers utilize a blue screen to make the animal "appear" to be in an unsafe place. For example, to give the appearance that the tiger in *Dr. Dolittle* is on a dangerous ledge, they filmed the animal against a blue background and then **superimposed** its image onto the desired setting.

In **predator-prey** scenes, filmmakers use a split screen. They film the animals separately, then join the film together to make it appear as if they are together on the screen. The movie *Homeward Bound: The Incredible Journey,* for example, applied the split-screen method. In this film, a cat and two dogs travel over miles of mountainous country to find their way home. In the scenes where the three animals meet wild animals such as a skunk, bear, and mountain lion, the "enemy" animals are filmed separately from the three "heroes." Then film editors cut the film and **spliced** it together. In reality, the animals were never near one another.

Talking Animals

A palomino horse named Mr. Ed was the first "talking" animal on television. The secret of how the trainer induced Mr. Ed appear to talk was a thin nylon line that ran through the horse's mouth. Whenever Ed was suppose to talk, the trainer pulled the nylon line and Ed began moving his lips, trying to dislodge it. This suc-

The stars of Homeward Bound: The Incredible Journey *set off on their travels.*

cessful half-hour television comedy series lasted for 143 episodes.

Today filmmakers achieve the illusion of talking animals with computers. The film *Dr. Dolittle* used 2-D imaging, the newest method of creating the impression that the animals chat. They filmed the animals with their mouths moving naturally. In postproduction, editors skillfully manipulated the mouth movements frame by frame to make it seem as if the animal were forming the words with its own lips, tongue, and teeth. The movie *Babe,* in contrast, used superimposed computer-generated motions over the animal actors' mouths to make it seem like the animals were having conversations.

Chapter Four

Television Acting

Today four-legged actors appear regularly on television situation comedies as well as in many **commercials**. Time commitment is a consideration for animal actors as well as human actors. If an animal is in a weekly television sitcom, the animal goes to the set only one day a week.

A Television Series

Moose, a Jack Russell terrier, portrays Eddie in the TV comedy series *Frasier*. Moose's story is one of overnight success, and he has been propelled to a fame like megastars Lassie and Rin Tin Tin. Moose is one of ten pups and learned to perform by hand signals at Canine Corral in Florida. He auditioned at Universal Studios in Orlando and has been on *Frasier* since 1994. Moose lives in Florida and California with his mate, Molly, and their two pups.

Animals in Commercials

Advertisers have found that animals grab viewers' attention and sell products. Thus, many animals are in demand for short-term jobs, such as television commercials.

For commercials, casting directors usually hire at least two animals for any given acting job—one to star and one to act as a backup, in case anything goes wrong with the star. Both animals earn the same amount of money, but only one is seen on TV.

In pet food commercials, the animal is hired first, then human actors audition to see how well they get along with

Moose the Jack Russell terrier became a megastar after his 1994 debut on Frasier.

the star. One actress, auditioning for a cat food commercial, showed up with a bit of tuna tucked into her cheek. When the cat nuzzled her cheek, she was immediately hired.

Filming a pet food commercial is a difficult job. Sherri Kaiserman, a trainer at New York's Dawn Animal Agency, says: "Sometimes, if [the animals] don't like the [advertised] food, we wait until the client's back is turned, then we put the animal's own food in the bowl—just underneath the product. Then [the animals will] eat it."[5]

Taco Bell Chihuahua

From 1997 until 2000, a Chihuahua named Gidget pitched tacos, chalupas, gorditas, and other Mexican dishes on TV and in print ads for Taco Bell. Filmmakers changed Gidget's facial expression by using a digital animated eyebrow and made her mouth appear to move by adding a mechanical jaw line to her image. The whole campaign was shot in about four days on location in Los Angeles. All film was shot and photos taken with the dogs (Gidget and her double) in costume on a perfectly white soundstage. The crowds, the location, the sound, the computer graphics, and the voice-overs were added later.

Gidget the Chihuahua starred in Taco Bell ads.

Commercials with Cats

A dog works to please its trainer. But a cat works to please itself. A cat needs to think it is doing what it wants to do, not what the trainer wants it to do.

Morris the cat was famous for his 9-Lives cat food commercials. Morris was a TV

Morris the cat became a famous TV personality from ads for 9-Lives cat food.

personality, not an actor. He did not do tricks. Morris coolly walked off the set when he decided he was finished acting for the day. The voice-overs for Morris's commercials were done before the ads were filmed. Morris was matched up to the dialogue. The two cats that have played the aloof Morris in his fifty-four different 9-Lives commercials have been fourteen-pound cats. Both of the salmon-orange tiger cats were rescued from animal shelters. The name Morris was inspired by the M-shaped mark on the cat's forehead.

Another cat, Gimmel, is familiar to millions as the finicky cat in the Fancy Feast cat food commercials. The silver-pointed Persian cat also acted as the double for Snowbell in the *Stuart Little* movie.

Mr. Ed and Big Red won PATSY awards for outstanding performances in movies and TV.

PATSY Awards

As with human actors, Hollywood wanted to honor animal actors and their trainers. From 1951 to 1986, the American Humane Association gave a yearly "Animal Oscar," called a PATSY Award. PATSY stands for Picture Animal Top Star of the Year. The award recognized animal stars who gave outstanding performances in motion pictures, television, and commercials. Some of the winners were Morris the cat, Lassie, Rin Tin Tin, Big Red, Benji, and Mr. Ed. AHA stopped awarding the PATSYs due to lack of funding.

Whether or not the animal actors are award winners, they continue to entertain us. And they are fortunate to have the American Humane Association on the sets to protect their interests. Trainers, owners, and the viewing public all benefit from animal actors.

Epilogue

Between Jobs

Animal actors, like most human actors, usually do not have a job to go to every day. When not acting, making personal appearances, or visiting schools for educational programs, most domestic animals, such as cats, dogs, and birds, live ordinary lives at home with their owners or trainers.

Mr. Jiggs the Chimpanzee

Mr. Jiggs is one of a dozen chimps who has played Cheetah in *Tarzan* movies. Mr. Jiggs also makes TV appearances and entertains at parties, weddings, bar mitzvahs, and schools. Mr. Jiggs lives with his owner Ronald Winters. The chimp has a good life, as described in a magazine article:

> Mr. Jiggs goes to sleep at six at night and doesn't wake up till about eight in the morning. Mr. Jiggs sleeps in his own double bed, in his own bedroom, in Mr. Winters' home, in Ramsey, New Jersey. In his bedroom [Mr. Jiggs] also has his own refrigerator and his own smoke detector. "If Jiggs' smoke detector goes off," Mr. Winters said, "he'll automatically open the window to his bedroom and go down an

Mr. Jiggs, Cheetah in Tarzan, *made TV appearances and entertained at parties.*

escape ladder to the back yard. . . . He's never been in a cage. He's always lived right in my house."[6]

Other Lodgings for Exotic Animals

However, most exotic or wild animals need special places to live. Some live on a ranch or **sanctuary**. Lloyd Beebe developed Walt Disney's Olympic Game Farm, a preserve paradise near Sequim, Washington, where Disney animals go when they are not working.

The Olympic Game Farm allows exotic animals such as tigers, bears, deer, zebras, and buffalo to roam uncaged, while enjoying some of the same scenic pleasures they would enjoy in the wild. Near the ocean and away from populated cities, this geographic location offers breezy unpolluted air and scenery of firs, cedars, and vegetation that is more interesting than any zoo could offer. There is no concrete, only earth covered with fragrant fir, bark, and grass.

Walt Disney's Olympic Game Farm houses
wild animal actors when they are not working.

A Group of Buildings Enclosed by a Barrier

Other animals may stay at a compound, where they live in large oversize cages. Bob Dunn's two-acre compound is staffed by two keepers and five trainers. At the compound all animals, from the **primates** (monkeys and apes) to birds to small animals, such as squirrels and prairie dogs, are given daily behavioral "enrichments" to keep them busy.

A capuchin monkey and a keeper enjoy a playful moment.

For example, the capuchin monkeys' enrichments include nuts to crack open and branches, which they use to make nests and holes in the ground or to weave through the bars of their cages. They also munch on leaves and berries from the branches. Dunn's four capuchin monkeys live together in one spacious cage, measuring about twenty feet long by fifteen feet wide and ten feet tall. The capuchins are brought indoors each night and put in individual crates.

The chimpanzees and other apes are moved to different cages each day so they have a change of scenery, and they are moved into a temperature-controlled building at night. Birds also sleep indoors during cold weather. Whether on or off the job, animal actors are usually well taken care of, humanely trained, and loved.

Notes

Chapter 2: Training Animal Actors

1. Quoted in John Javna, *Animal Superstars*. Milwaukee: Hal Leonard Books, 1986, p. 58.
2. Ralph Helfer, *The Beauty of the Beasts*. Los Angeles: Jeremy P. Tarcher, 1990, p. 56.
3. Quoted in Tala Skari, "A New Movie of Unbearable Suspense," *Life*, Spring 1989, pp. 89–90.

Chapter 3: Animals on the Job

4. Quoted in Emily D'Aulaire, "Animal Stars," *Good Housekeeping*, May 1989, pp. 60–62.

Chapter 4: Television Acting

5. Quoted in Micki Siegel, "That's Show-Biz!" *Good Housekeeping*, February 1991, pp. 72–75.

Epilogue: Between Jobs

6. Quoted in *New Yorker*, "Trouper," April 14, 1986, pp. 30–31.

Glossary

animate: to give life to

audition: to try out for a part in a movie, TV show, or play

commercial: a radio or TV ad that aims to sell a product

compound: a group of buildings set off and enclosed by a barrier

domestic animal: a tame animal that can live in a family home

exotic animal: a wild or unusual animal from another part of the world

generation: descending offspring from common parents

gorge: to eat greedily

humane: in a kind manner

predator: an animal that preys upon others

prey: an animal hunted or caught for food; a victim

primates: monkeys and apes

rehabilitate: to restore useful life through therapy and education

repetition: doing something over and over

sanctuary: place of protection for animals

sill: the flat bottom of a window frame

simulate: to pretend or fake

splice: to join at the ends

superimpose: to lay or place on or over something else

venomous: poisonous

vinyl: a type of flexible plastic

Organizations to Contact

American Humane Association
15366 Dickens St.
Sherman Oaks, CA 91403
(888) 301-3541
www.AHAfilm.org
Site gives reviews of movies that have animal actors, AHA history and guidelines, and animal information.

Bob Dunn's Animal Services
16001 Yarnell St.
Sylmar, CA 91342
(818) 896-0394
www.animalservices.com
Site shows colored photos of all available animals from Dunn's Services: birds, cats, dogs, apes, exotics, insects, hoofstock, monkeys, reptiles, and rodents.

Dawn Animal Agency
750 Eighth Ave.
New York, NY 10036
(212) 575-9396
www.dawnanimalagency.com
Shows photos of animals available for acting jobs.

Vital Ground
P.O. Box 982003
Park City, UT 84098
(435) 658-0009
www.vitalground.org
Shows scenes of Tank the Bear in *Dr. Dolittle 2,* photos of "Little" Bart the Bear and Honey-Bump Bear, and a tribute in memory of Bart the Bear.

For Further Exploration

John Javna, *Animal Superstars.* Milwaukee: Hal Leonard Books, 1986. Looks at many performing animals primarily in films and on TV, such as Benji, Flipper, Gentle Ben, Lassie, Mr. Ed, Morris the cat, and Rin Tin Tin.

Gary Paulsen and Art Browne Jr., *TV and Movie Animals.* New York: Julian Messner, 1980. Discusses the use of animals in films and television, including their training and a typical shooting day on the set.

Elaine Scott, *Safe in the Spotlight.* New York: Morrow, 1991. Explains how the Sanctuary for Animals and the Dawn Animal Agency hire out healthy animals for jobs in the performing arts and then use the money to support other animals at the sanctuary who are too old or too sick to work themselves.

Index

Picture Credits

Cover: © Matthew Klein
© AFP/CORBIS, 5, 17
Associated Press/Buena Vista Pictures, 29
Associated Press/Standard-Examiner, 19
Associated Press/Universal Studios, 25
© Bettmann/CORBIS, 7, 8, 20, 33, 34
© Anna Clopet/CORBIS, 22
© Gallo Images/CORBIS, 16
© Shelley Gazin/CORBIS, 23
© Mitchell Gerber/CORBIS, 31, 32
© Darrell Gulin/CORBIS, 37
© David G. Houser/CORBIS, 14
© Archive Photos, 36
© Tom Nebbia/CORBIS, 13
© Jeffrey L. Rotman/CORBIS, 11, 38
© Nancy R. Schiff/Archive Photos, 9
© James A. Sugar/CORBIS, 27
© Randy Wells/CORBIS, 26

About the Author

Judith Janda Presnall is an award-winning nonfiction writer. Her books include *Rachel Carson, Artificial Organs, The Giant Panda, Oprah Winfrey, Mount Rushmore, Life on Alcatraz, Animals That Glow, Animal Skeletons,* and *Circuses.* Presnall graduated from the University of Wisconsin in Whitewater. She is a recipient of the Jack London Award for meritorious service in the California Writers Club. She is also a member of the Society of Children's Book Writers and Illustrators. She lives in the Los Angeles area with her husband Lance.